How WWII Transformed Women's Style in the US.

Ronald L. Vick

ABSTRACT

World War II (hereafter referred to as WWII) is a fascinating era in fashion, society, and politics. The fashion of the era was truly representative of the events happening in the world in a most visible way. This era made indelible marks on future designers and the science of fashion as the world knows it. Fashion and costume design were influenced and changed due to the many limitations presented and imposed by WWII. WWII represents a great marker of change socially, technologically, economically, and politically. While it affected the entire world, the main focus of this thesis will explore the effect of WWII on fashion and costume design on the United States and Britain.

Due to the war-time restrictions of raw materials, as well as bans on some imported materials, man-made fibers were created and popularized. The impact of the war was seen not only in fabric choices but also in the style and silhouette of the clothing. There was a new simplicity seen in women's clothing that required designers and everyday women to tap into their imagination and make the government mandates fashionable.

The silhouette lines of the clothing produced in this period are still found in clothing today, as are the man-made materials which were developed during the war. Because of rationing and unavailability of materials, the differences in social classes were not as visibly noticeable, as the dress and style of all women became similar under government mandates. This was reflected in the style of dress for work, formal events, and on the silver screen in Hollywood. This thesis will prove WWII imposed sociological and aesthetic limitations on fashion in the U.S. and Britain.

TABLE OF CONTENTS

Abstract..iii

Table of Contents..iv

List of Tables..v

List of Figures...vi

Chapter One: Historic Overview: A Snapshot of the World at Large from 1920-1940..........1

Chapter Two: How WWII Impacted Fashion with its Limitations................................6

Chapter Three: The War's Influence on the Entertainment Industry from Hollywood to Broadway..26

Chapter Four: The Beginning of a Synthetic Revolution in Fashion..............................41

Chapter Five: Designers that made an Impact during the War..47

Conclusion..62

Bibliography...64

Works Cited..70

Curriculum Vitae..72

LIST OF TABLES

Table 1: Coupon Values for Women, Courtesy of Fashion-Era.com 10

LIST OF FIGURES

Figure 1: Ration Book, UK, c. 1942, contributed by Hazel Banney..8

Figure 2: CC41 Utility Clothing Label, from a 1940's Ermine-look Rabbit Fur Coat....................11

Figure 3: WWII Utility Clothing for women, c. 1942, Photograph by James Jarche.....................11

Figure 4: Example of a Utility dress, rayon, English, 1942, Victoria and Albert Museum...............13

Figure 5: Winston Churchill and his famous "V", c. 1941, London...14

Figure 6: "Swing Kids", Hamburg, Germany, c. 1939..15

Figure 7: *Les Zazous*, Illustration, c. 1942, Paris..16

Figure 8: *VOGUE* magazine cover, January 1942. U.S..17

Figure 9: Lane Bryant Catalog Advertisement, c 1943, Indiana...19

Figure 10: Raffia and Cork Wedge, Salvatore Ferragamo, c.1943...21

Figure 11: Kay Bensel Applying Stocking Seams with Contraption, c. 1942, Kitsch-Slapped.com.....22

Figure 12: Woman's Own, Women's Hat Portraits, 1945, U.K., Gliclee Print..............................23

Figure 13: Veronica Lake, Publicity Photo for *This Gun for Hire*, 1942....................................25

Figure 14: Ingrid Bergman in *Casablanca*, wearing a White suit with Clip Broach, 1943, Hollywood..27

Figure 15: Makeup Advertisement for Elizabeth Arden, c. 1943, Courtesy of the Advertising Archives..30

Figure 16: Max Factor Advertisement, c. 1943, Hollywood, CA..31

Figure 17: "Liquid" Stockings, courtesy of Simonleblanc.com..32

Figure 18: Above: Before- Max Factor Packaging made of metal and glass, c. 1935.

        Photo taken at the Max Factor Museum, Hollywood, CA................................33

Figure 19: After: Max Factor Packaging made mostly of plastic, c. 1942.

        Photo taken at the Max Factor   Museum, Hollywood, CA.............................34

Figure 20: British Ad for "Tangee" Lip color, c. 1943, London..35

Figure 21: Betty Grable in "Victory Rolls", c. 1943..36

Figure 22: Factory workers wearing Snoods, c. 1942...37

Figure 23: Ad for *Warner's Hollywood Canteen*, c. 1944, Hollywood......................................38

Figure 24: *Stage Door Canteen* Movie Poster, Sol Lesser Productions, 1943...........................39

Figure 25: Elsa Schiaparelli's "Glass Cape", 1934, Paris..42

Figure 26: Poster for the New York World Fair, 1939..45

Figure 27: Coco Chanel (left) and a friend wearing her Jersey Knit Suit...................................48

Figure 28: Coco Chanel's "Little Black Dress", 1926, Paris...49

Figure 29: Bow-knot Sweater, Hand-knit pullover sweater with bow-knot, November 1927,

        Black and White Wool, by Elsa Schiaparelli..50

Figure 30: "*Shoe Hat*" by Elsa Schialparelli, collaboration with Salvador Dali,

        Black Wook Felt, 1937-38..52

Figure 31: Vintage Advertisement for the Gossard Line of Beauty, c. 1931..............................54

Figure 32: Joan Crawford in Letty Lynton, Designed by Adrian, 1932, Hollywood...................55

Figure 33: Suit by Adrian, c. 1944, Hollywood..56

Figure 34: Mainbocher's Uniform Design for the U.S. Navy's WAVES, 1942..........................57

Figure 35: WASP Uniforms, c. 1944, courtesy of the Army Air Corps Library and Museum..........58

Figure 36: "*Salvage Your Rubber*", Jacqmar Propaganda Scarf, early 1940's,

        Paul and Karen Renny Collection...59

Figure 37: Veronica Lake in the Night Gown designed by Edith Head for *I Married a Witch*, 1942...60

Chapter One

A Historic Overview: A Snapshot of the World at Large from 1920-1940

It is important to understand the context in which the world conducted itself before and during WWII, and why the citizens of the U.S. and Britain were so affected in their clothing fashion, and in day to day life. The fashions of the time were absolutely reflections of the economy and the state of the political world. The following is a snapshot of the events leading up to WWII and the effects those events had on fashion.

In the World War I, the Allies (the United States of America, France, Britain, Belgium, Italy, Japan, and Russia) fought against the Central Powers (Germany, Austria-Hungary, Turkey and Bulgaria). At the end of WWI, in 1918, The Treaty of Versailles was drawn. This peace settlement stated that Germany was at fault for starting WWI and therefore was responsible for the damage caused. The Central powers were to pay reparations to the Allies and were also forced to sign separate treaties that penalized them in different ways.

During the 1920's Germany fulfilled its obligations as demanded by the Treaty of Versailles. In order to make reparations, Germany took a loan from the U.S., and in order to make the payments, it relied on international trade, especially with the U.S. This is an important fact, because even though the U.S. was insistent on repayment, in 1922 it passed considerably high tariffs on imported goods, which made international trade difficult, and therefore nearly impossible for reparation payments to be made. Then, in 1929 the U.S. stock market crashed, sending the U.S. into the Great Depression. Because of the loans the U.S. had made to the rest of the world, including Allies, the Great Depression was eventually felt worldwide.

Japan, being on the Allies' side during WWI, was closely allied with Britain and expected to receive the spoils of war as did the other victor nations. However, Japan felt unrecognized by the Western Powers as the dominant force in the Pacific. The sense of discrimination against those of color, and in particular, Asians, was apparent in the United States with such acts passed as the 1913 Alien Land Law in which Asian immigrants could not purchase nor lease land. This law was again passed in 1920 after WWI. Japan had proposed a Racial Equality Clause for the League of Nations Charter in 1919 which was rejected. Even though the U.S. did not join the League of Nations, U.S. President Woodrow Wilson was the chairman of the committee for the creation of the League. He, along with Britain and France, opposed the Racial Equality Clause and therefore added to the ever-growing tension between the Western powers and Japan.

In the late 19th and early 20th centuries, Japan had won territory in China as a result of two wars, one with China and one with Russia. In this, Japan took control of parts of Manchuria (Eastern China) and Korea. This was important because of the lack of raw materials in Japan. By the 1930's, with Japan in control of certain parts of China, they also controlled the raw materials in that area and therefore the trade of those materials: most importantly, rubber.

At the writing of the Treaty of Versailles, the U.S. urged Japan to concede parts of China so that there would be open trade between countries and less imperialism. Japan agreed, but kept a military presence in China. This agreement with the U.S. allowed Japan's industrial production to double, and exports increased with 40 percent going to the United States (Adams 29).

With the Great Crash of the U.S. stock market in 1929, the export business between Japan and the U.S. plummeted; the raw silk industry alone fell 65% in one year (Adams 29). The U.S. then implemented the Smoot-Hawley Tariff which raised import taxes by 50%. "Overall, world trade declined by some 66%, between 1929 and 1934. More generally, Smoot-Hawley did nothing to foster trust and cooperation among nations in either the political or economic realm during a perilous era in international relations" (U.S. Dept. of State). The Tariff was initially implemented to try and help preserve the U.S. economy at home. It really did nothing except provoke other nations further into a depression and into a more militaristic stance while projecting a stronger image of U.S. isolationism. It prompted the Japanese to react by reengaging in a militaristic way. Japan now identified themselves with the other self-proclaimed "have-not" nations: Germany and Italy. Italy, too, was expecting more spoils from the Treaty of Versailles. Instead they returned from WWI with a depressed economy, high unemployment, and a reduced naval fleet in the Mediterranean. Benito Mussolini rose to power as the dictator of Italy in 1922. He wanted to gain the respect, land, and reparations he felt was due to his country that the Treaty of Versailles ignored. He introduced Fascism--a governmental system led by a dictator having complete power; forcibly suppressing opposition and criticism; regimenting all industry, commerce, etc.; and emphasizing an aggressive nationalism and often racism.

With the decline of the German economy as well, Adolf Hitler, a charismatic political leader emerged. He declared that Germany would no longer take the blame for WWI, that reparation payments would be stopped, and that land he believed belonged to Germany would be taken back. He formed the Nazi party and in 1933 became Chancellor of Germany. "Hitler became a social Darwinist of the simplest and most dangerous kind, dedicated to German survival through the national adoption of military values and goals" (Adams 32). Hitler admired Mussolini's Fascism and duplicated the style of dictatorship.

"These three countries recognized German hegemony over most of continental Europe; Italian hegemony over the Mediterranean Sea; and Japanese hegemony over East Asia and the Pacific" (United States Holocaust Memorial Museum). In this way, Italy, Japan and Germany formed an alliance which was named the Axis Powers.

In 1937, Japan attacked China in a full-scale battle, upsetting the U.S. and their trade interests with a semi-independent China. The Second World War threatened to shift the rubber wealth. With Japan occupying prime rubber-producing areas in Southeast Asia, the U.S. feared it would run out of the vital material. Every tire, hose, seal, valve, and inch of wiring required rubber, along with rubber used for fashion. Silk was also a commodity of Japan that would become scarce once the war began, as Japan was the largest supplier in the world.

In September 1939, Germany invaded Poland and WWII began when Britain and France declared war on Germany. Perhaps one of the most important events to happen regarding fashion was the invasion and occupation of Paris on June 14, 1940 by Nazi Germany. Paris was the pinnacle and center of the fashion world until that time. The rest of the world looked towards it to establish the trends that would spread and become popular. Important fashion houses such as Chanel, Jean Patou, Jeanne Lanvin, and Elsa Schiaparelli maintained their headquarters in Paris. Most of the designers fled the country upon France's declaration of war in 1939. Others closed shop, and still others remained open; and with the occupation in 1940, they were cut off from the rest of the world. With Paris being in isolation, the fashion world had a gap which the U.S. and

Britain filled. This would be the first time a country other than France would be the driving force behind the fashions.

The U.S. supported its Allies by supplying materials to make ammunition, building war ships and through monetary lending. President Franklin Delano Roosevelt (1882-1945) proposed and then helped to pass the Lend-Lease Act in 1941. "In the 1940 Presidential election campaign, Roosevelt promised to keep America out of the war. He stated, 'I have said this before, but I shall say it again and again and again; your boys are not going to be sent into any foreign wars.' Nevertheless, FDR wanted to support Britain and believed the United States should serve as a 'great arsenal of democracy'" (Lend Lease Act 1941). The plan for the U.S. to maintain its isolation from the war was derailed in December of 1941 when Pearl Harbor was bombed.

Because of the help given to the Allies, the rationing of materials in both the U.S. and U.K. began as early as 1940. Metals that were used in clothing such as fasteners, boning for corsets, and zippers were all allocated to be used for the military. This allowed new innovations in science and fashion design to develop, mainly in the area of synthetic materials used for daily life and fashion. When the U.S. did finally enter WWII after the bombing of Pearl Harbor, rationing then greatly affected the general population.

Chapter Two

How WWII Impacted Fashion

Rationing was mandated by the each country's government, and was embraced and carried out by citizens the world over. It allowed for creativity to blossom under less than ideal conditions and brought people together for a cause. Events and inventions prior to WWII made the rationing program and lifestyle run more smoothly.

The Industrial Revolution which began in the late 1700's allowed the advancement of the mechanization of factories and the textile industry throughout the 1800's. The need for uniforms in the U.S. Civil War was the catalyst for men's ready-to-wear clothing in the 1860s. Millions of measurements were taken from the Civil War soldiers which allowed a ready-to-wear sizing system to be more available. In time, women's sizing was also developed. With the development of WWI, the ready-to-wear manufacturing of clothing also advanced in technology and speed; again, mainly for uniforms.

Even with the advancement of technology in the textile factories, at the beginning of the 20th century, most clothing was still either made in the home for those in the lower classes, or custom made for those of the upper classes. In the 1800's the garment industry expanded greatly. However, the styles of clothing were changing at a faster pace than before. Information from different parts of the world regarding fashion and trend traveled quicker due to international publications of magazines such as *VOGUE*. Originally founded in the U.S. in 1909, by 1920, *VOGUE* had international publication in Britain and France. Because of this, the clothing silhouette began to change as quickly as every 10 years. In comparison, with the technology we have today, trends change several times a year.

Transportation was a major influence in the changing fashions in the beginning of the 20th century. With bicycles becoming increasingly more popular for leisure activities in the early part of the century, and automobiles gaining popularity after 1908 (when Henry Ford introduced the automobile assembly line), clothing adapted accordingly by making ensembles to accompany the new forms of transportation. Women during WWI wore split skirts to travel to and from work, changing into more appropriate wear when necessary. It was a precursor to the practical clothing that would become a part of women's everyday work-wear during WWII.

Britain:

War was not a new way of life for the women and men of Britain. In WWI women were called to the factories and fields as the men went to battle. Uniforms for women during WWI resembled the military lines of the men. Women wore trousers while at work for the Land Army and in the munitions factories. Norfolk jackets, initially created for men, were tailored for women. Social stigmas were more prevalent during WWI and for the most part women did wear long skirts as part of their uniforms, unless it would impede upon their war-time occupation. When WWII began, the women of Britain, who for some had already been through WWI, once again donned their war-time uniforms in an updated fashion to for the war effort.

Before England declared war on Germany, the British government had been preparing for upcoming problems and shortages the country might face during the conflict. In September of 1939 a National Registration of the British population was held in order to issue identification cards needed for upcoming rationing coupon books as well to ensure a draft was available. In England, food was rationed first in January 1940. A year later clothing rationing was introduced along with a program to cover all problem areas: Rationing, Utility, and Austerity.

"Once an ID card was issued, a ration coupon book was issued with it. Given were 66 points for clothing per year to begin. In 1942 it was cut to 48 and in 1943 to 36, and in 1945 to 24. Children aged 14–16 got 20 more coupons to compensate for outgrowing clothes quickly. Clothing rationing points could be used for wool, cotton and household textiles. People had extra points for work clothes, such as overalls for factory work" (Rationing in the UK). (see fig.1)

Figure 1: Ration Book, UK, c. 1942, contributed by Hazel Banney.

In January 1941, a ban on silk for civilian clothing came into effect. Rubber and silk disappeared as they were mainly imported from Japan. Silk was needed for the making of parachutes, some of which would be used to send women spies, part of the Special Operations Executive (SOE), into German-occupied France to help with the French resistance and to retrieve information for the Allies. Shortages were also caused by Hitler's tactic to use submarines, or U-Boats, to bomb supply ships coming into Britain. The western world--- cut off from many resources--- had to eventually replace them by having The Women's Land Army (WLA) work the land to produce supplies such as food, and had to ration what was left. In Britain, things such as Kleenex (or any facial tissue) were hard to come by because of the lack of materials. Mollie Weinstein Schaffer, a U.S. member of the Women's Army Corps (WAC) stationed in London wrote to her family: "Here is a tip- when packing use Kleenex as a stuffer. Kleenex is rather difficult to get around here" (Schaffer 51).

The British government banned civilians from importing clothing from outside of Britain. They risked being fined if caught doing so. This was to ensure money for clothing would fund the British war effort. This is similar to the U.S. creating an isolated economy by placing such high tariffs on imports in order to make their own economy self-reliable.

In clothing rationing, maternity wear was not considered so alterations would need to be made to existing clothes or larger sizes needed to be bought. Many non-military employers did not provide work-wear, including shoes and uniforms, so that was a part of many household rations as well. However, there were extra coupons for factory work clothes such as coveralls. Below is an example of how many coupons were needed for different articles of clothing. (see table 1)

ITEM OF CLOTHING	WOMEN	GIRLS
Lined Mackintosh or Coat over 28"	14	11
Under 28" Short Coat or Jacket	11	8
Frock, Gown or Dress of Wool	11	8
Frock, Gown or Dress of Other Fabric	7	5
Bodice with girl's skirt or Gym Tunic	8	6
Pajamas	8	6
Divided Skirt or Skirt [Full]	7	5
Nightdress	6	5
Dungarees or Overalls	6	4
Blouse, Shirt, Sports top, Cardigan	5	3
Pair of Slippers, Boots, Shoes	5	3
Other Garments including Corsets	5	2
Petticoat, Slip, Knickers/combo	4	3
Apron or Pinafore	3	2
Scarf, gloves, mittens or muff	2	2
Stockings per pair	2	1
Ankle Socks per pair	1	1
1 yard wool cloth 36" wide	3	3
2 ounces of wool knitting yarn	1	1

Table 1: Coupon Values for Women, Courtesy of Fashion-Era.com

The *Utility Scheme*, as it came to be known, was a plan that reduced the range of clothing available. It helped to concentrate efforts on the production of textiles that would wear and clean well. Textiles had a regulated price and did not have a sales tax. One thing the *Utility Scheme* did was help to improve ready-to-wear clothing in Britain by streamlining industrial made clothing. It was an industry that was making a relatively small portion of clothing in the ready-to-wear capacity. The streamlining of clothing by rationing forced the industry to grow considerably and become uniform. With this streamlining, processes were developed to create garments more efficiently and swiftly which would be maintained and progress after the war. Under the *Utility Scheme*, a Utility Apparel order required all garments to be labeled "CC41 (Civilian Clothing 1941)." (see fig.2)

Figure 2: CC41 Utility Clothing Label, from a 1940's Ermine-look Rabbit Fur Coat.

Clothing prices more than doubled between 1939 and 1941 due to availability of supplies. With this problem, women of middle to lower classes were finding it more difficult to obtain quality clothing and undergarments that would last them through the war. Utility clothing provided a way to control prices.

Figure 3: WWII Utility Clothing for women, c. 1942, Photograph by James Jarche.

The Board of Trade, which regulated retail trade, consolidated the number of factories that produced civilian clothing. Incentives were given to those factories that used 75% or more of their capital for Utility clothes. In 1942, 50 % of the clothing produced was under the *Utility Scheme*. By the end of the war that number had jumped to 85%. Incentives included a larger amount of raw material and textiles from which to make the clothing and a promise that no more workers would be taken from their factory for deployment. (see fig. 3)

In January 1942, The Board of Trade and London's Fashion Group, which was made up of London's more prominent designers, joined forces at the prompting of *British VOGUE's* editor, Alison Settle, to create the Incorporated Society of London's Fashion Designers. It came to be known as Inc. Soc. The group's purpose was to band together London's designers like Paris' Haute Couture Syndicate. It was commissioned by The Board of Trade to create a suit, a dress, and an overcoat under the Utility specifications but with more appeal to the general public. The Inc. Soc. was given the rations of fabric as follows: overcoat- 2 ¾ yards, dress- 2 yards, suit- 2 ½ yards. Thirty-two designs were presented and deemed a great success. The new designs offered simplicity in style, were wearable and comfortable, yet had an elegance about them which was greatly appreciated by the public. In Britain's attempt to create and maintain a national hold on fashion (and therefore a steady income to help fund the war) and create a unified front, individual designers were not noted during the presentation of the designs. (see fig. 4)

Figure 4: Example of a Utility dress, rayon, English, 1942, Victoria and Albert Museum.

The other purpose for the Inc. Soc.'s designing was to show the United States that Britain was an excellent and talented option for exports in fashion during the war and after. Britain wouldn't allow imports of clothing but was excited about exporting. With Paris under the occupation of Nazi Germany, Parisian designers were no longer in the forefront of the fashion world; Britain wanted to take their place. The Inc. Soc. did obtain success even after the war, with exports being five times what they were before the war (Walford). Utility clothing continued to be made in Britain until 1952 which was much longer than the duration of wartime fashion in the U.S.

The set of directives known as *Austerity* were applied to all clothing including custom work. While the *Utility Scheme* set rules for yardage and who was able to manufacture clothing, the *Austerity* directives set rules for *how* a garment is made. There was to be no superfluous décor, which is why it was named the *Austerity* directives. Rules included:

- Jackets and Coats could have no more than 3 pockets
- Dresses may only have 2 pockets
- No metal or leather buttons
- No boys under 13 could wear long trousers
- No tail coats
- All braid, embroidery, and lace were banned
- Corset manufacturers were prohibited from using shirring, ruching or fancy stitching on women's underwear.

In 1944 some restrictions were lifted with victory in sight: pleats and buttons on shirt were permitted and men could wear cuffed trousers once more (Walford).

Figure 5: Winston Churchill and his famous "V", c. 1941, London.

The patriotism shown in Britain was outstanding. The "V for VICTORY" campaign which was devised by Victor De Lavelaye, head of the Belgian Service of the BBC, was devised in 1941. (see fig. 5) Winston Churchill popularized the slogan with his upheld fingers in the shape of a "V". The slogan and the capital "V" were found on everything from patriotic jewelry to food packaging.

Figure 6: "Swing Kids", Hamburg, Germany, c. 1939.

Britain's fashion was influential around the world, especially men's fashion as it influenced the rebellious youth of Germany known as "Swing Kids", in wearing what the German officials deemed frivolous and un-German. (see fig. 6) In the late 1930's in Germany, the Swing Kids carried umbrellas with them with no regard to the actual weather, wore their hair longer to mimic the jazz artists of the day, and carried an opinion of liberation with them that they found admirable in the British and American men. Churchill was one of the figures they emulated. In France, the rebellious group that emulated British and American fashions were known as the *Zazous*. The group is said to have been named after the famous Cab Calloway jazz song *"Zaz Zuh Zaz,"* which was indicative of what the group strived for fashion-wise. They were considered to be a rebellious group, very disliked by the Nazi regime, who believed in all things anti-war. (see fig. 7) The women wore makeup and bright red lipstick, colored their hair to be like the Hollywood blonde bomb shells, and wore fitted sweaters with brightly printed skirts and socks.

Figure 7 "Les Zazous", Illustration, c. 1942, Paris.

The Nazi party pushed for women to return to matronly styles with very minimal styling of clothing, hair, and makeup; the *Zazous* were the anti-thesis of this. They listened to American Jazz music, fashioned themselves after the starlets of the silver screen, and avoided anything that had to do with the war if possible. Seen as degenerates and disrespectful, the Nazis persecuted them and put them in labor camps outside of the city. Through fashion they expressed their distaste for the regime and their loyalty to freedom and beauty.

United States:

In December 1941 the United States officially entered WWII after the bombing of Pearl Harbor. Fashion design came to a halt. "President Franklin Roosevelt ordered the War Production Board (hereafter referred to as WPB), whose purpose…was to regulate the production and allocation of materials and fuel' (Board) to change the nation's economy to better suit the war" (Rationing Fashion in the U.S.). The U.S., having maintained a relative distance from WWI until the end of the war, was not as versed in war-time fashion changes as Britain.

Maintaining beauty and allure were major war-time challenges faced by designers. American *VOGUE* magazine's first cover for January after the U.S. entry into the war spoke of the new life American women would have to face and how to look gorgeous while doing it. (see fig. 8)

Figure 8: *VOGUE* magazine cover, January 1942. U.S.

"The first nonfood item rationed was rubber. The Japanese had seized plantations in the Dutch East Indies that produced 90% of America's raw rubber. President Roosevelt called on citizens to help by contributing scrap rubber to be recycled, old tires, old rubber raincoats, garden hose, rubber shoes, bathing caps" (WWII Rationing on the U.S. Homefront).

Rationing in the U.S. was different from the U.K. and other European countries, including Germany, in that the responsibility of clothing rationing was on the manufacturers of clothing rather than civilians. Stanley Marcus (of Nieman Marcus) was the head of the textiles division of the WPB. He essentially froze the silhouette of the time by restricting the amount of fabric that could be used to create a garment to its 1941 amount (Walford).

Under Marcus and the WPB, rules for the garment industry were created such as L-85. The "L" stood for "Limitation Order" and was then followed by a number. L-85 covered women's clothing. There were very heavy fines and potential jail time for manufacturers that broke the rules set by the WPB.

Examples of L-85 mandates for manufacturers:

-Blouses:

-If tucking or pleating is used, ruffling cannot be used and vice versa.

-No hoods.

-No more than one pocket, inside or out, and no patch pocket using more than 25 square inches of material.

-Coats:

-No bi-swing or Norfolk type backs.

-No epaulets or tabs on the shoulder.

-Sleeve circumference is limited to 16 ½ inches.

-Skirts, Skirt Suits and Play Suits:

-Hem circumference reduced from 81 inches to 78 inches for a misses size 16 made in non-wool fabrics or in wool fabrics of a 9 ounce weight or less.

-No culottes, reversible skirts, lined skirts, quilted skirts or skating skirts.

-No waistband over 3 inches wide.

-Dresses:

-No more than 2 buttons and 2 buttonholes for each cuff.

- No quilting using more than 300 square inches.

-Evening Dresses: Sweep of taffeta, flat satin, and dresses of similar materials remains at 144 inches.

Civilians were limited to only 3 pairs of leather footwear per year. (see fig. 9) Shoes were rationed because an uncontrolled demand would have been much greater than the supply which had greatly decreased, because of leather and manpower shortages as well as military demand.

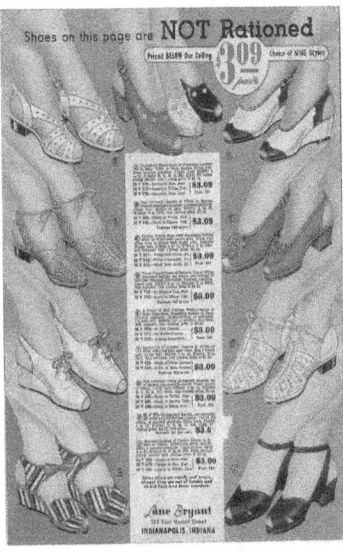

Figure 9: Lane Bryant Catalog Advertisement, c 1943, Indiana

"The shoe rationing program was a universal and systematic coupon program. By the use of stamps having no termination date, every individual was given the right to purchase a pair of shoes with each valid shoe stamp contained in his Ration Book #3. Shoe stamps were validated periodically. War ration shoe stamps were transferable between members of a family living together in the same household" (Kolkman). However, companies like Sears, Roebuck & Co. offered shoes for other rationing coupons. People could detach War Ration Stamp No. 17 from their War Ration Book No. 1 (sugar and coffee book) and pin it to their order. Other companies such as Lane Bryant ran advertisements for "Non-Rationed Shoes" which were shoes made of non-leather and were also of the wedge style or a combination of the two. Lane Bryant was a company offering practicality with a pleasant aesthetic. Alice Joyce Lee, who was 14 in 1942, recalled in my interview, that in Mobile, Alabama they were allowed 2 pairs of shoes per year. She had one pair for school and church and one for "bumping about" or play (Lee).

The Wedge shoe is another article of clothing that came into immense popularity during WWII due to rationing. Originally created by Salvatore Ferragamo in 1935, it used cork for the soles of the shoes instead of leather. This was extremely useful during wartime; the wedges that were created had wooden or cork soles and had fabric or a natural fiber such as hemp to make up the upper part of the shoe. (see fig. 10)

Figure 10: Raffia and Cork Wedge, Salvatore Ferragamo, c.1943.

Mendes and de la Haye said in their book, *20th Century Fashion*: "From 1940, when the use of leather was reserved exclusively for soldier's boots, Ferragamo's coulourful shoes, often featuring oriental upturned toes, utilized such diverse materials as hemp, felt, raffia and crocheted and plaited cellophane" (118).

The war had priority so the military need for materials such as wool and cotton had to be fulfilled first before they could be used for civilian clothing. As in the allied countries, silk and rubber were not available as early as the fall of 1941 in the U.S. because the last shipments leaving Japan were in August 1941. Nylon served as a replacement for silk for a short time in 1939; however, it became needed for the creation of parachutes, so women resorted to drawing black lines on the back of their legs in place of actual stockings, along with leg makeup. "Here, 1942 Hollywood starlet Kay Bensel applied her faux stocking seams with a device 'made from a screw driver handle, bicycle leg-clip, and an ordinary eyebrow pencil" (Deanna). (see fig. 11) The shortage of stockings did increase the popularity of the trouser which were mostly adopted by young women and working women.

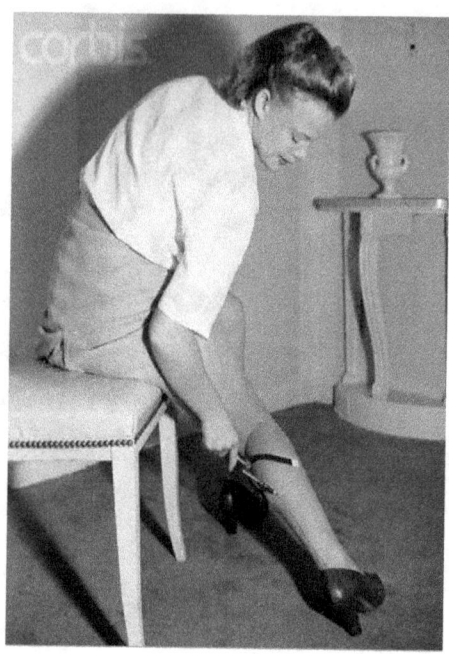

Figure 11: Kay Bensel Applying Stocking Seams with Contraption, c. 1942, Kitsch-Slapped.com

As stated earlier, women in Britain wore trousers as early as WWI due to their part in the workforce. The trouser as a regular item of clothing in a woman's wardrobe was not readily accepted until WWII in either Britain or the U.S. Popular film stars Katharine Hepburn and Marlene Dietrich wore them regularly in the 1930's and Coco Chanel before them with much controversy in the media. To society and to the women who donned them, trousers were a statement of independence and equality to that of men. It was not until they were essential to war-time efforts and jobs that most of society deemed them acceptable, and even then, preferred them worn only at work.

Because of the restrictions of L-85, American designers, although eager to make a place in the fashion world, were not allowed a huge margin for originality or drama in their designs. Millinery was not under ration and so many women sought their individuality using this accessory. Hats were at times whimsical and colorful and other times quite small, resembling men's hats and tended to have a military look to them. Propaganda was a large part of accessorizing as well. Pins with patriotic messages were added to clothing, hats, and scarves to jazz up women's outfits. These accessories helped maintain the united patriotic front encouraged by the government. (see fig. 12)

Figure 12: Woman's Own, Women's Hat Portraits, 1945, U.K., Gliclee Print.

Traditional feminine clothing such as stockings, lace, huge sweeping gowns, silk, etc., therefore hats became a way to express femininity while maintaining the war-time silhouette imposed upon them.

Rationing also affected the hair and makeup industry in both the U.S. and the U.K. For makeup, important ingredients such as glycerin, castor oil, alcohol and talcum powder were set aside for the war effort. Beauty magazines took the lead in writing articles on how to maintain your looks in trying times by printing advice such as:

-To maintain the shine in your hair, use a natural bristled brush and brush your hair, moving the natural oils throughout your hair, instead of using *Brillantine* (a popular hair oil used for shine.)

- Keep natural nails buffed to a shine if you do not have lacquer, and to use lacquer sparingly as it was in short supply. Perhaps use only for special occasions.

-Face creams became quite popular, especially with women who worked at the factories, because they helped to protect the skin from the toxins in the work environment.

As for hair, it became increasingly important to recycle hair pins, combs, or any other products made of metal. Max Factor, who besides having a successful makeup line, also had a wig making department. He was notoriously thrifty in his career before the war, and it helped his business during the war to continue to be that way. He would have his staff recycle all pins found on the ground during the styling and wig-making process. Clients would bring in their own container of pins if they wished to have their hair styled into an up-do. Veronica Lake made the deep side part and shoulder length hair extremely popular during the period. (see fig. 13) It was a style that was easily achieved by the everyday woman and starlets alike. It used little product and hair could be rolled in pin curls or with fabric.

Figure 13: Veronica Lake, Publicity Photo for *This Gun for Hire*, 1942.

The overwhelming desired result during this period was, despite rationing, to appear beautiful and strong, which in turn proved patriotism and support.

Chapter Three

The War's Influence on the Entertainment Industry from Hollywood to Broadway

To say that Hollywood impacted fashion during WWII in spite of restrictions is a huge understatement. Not only did it affect the image of the war on the U.S. home-front, its reach extended overseas to the U.K. and other Allied countries. Distribution even reached Germany for some films. Looking at how rationing and restricted access to materials affected production in Hollywood is really a look at how the entire war machine used and exempted the studios, actors and actresses to further the war effort.

The L-85 mandates did not really affect Hollywood studios in the way they did the rest of the fashion industry. Those particular mandates were intended for manufacturers of textiles and clothing during the war. If there were any new clothing that was purchased for a particular film, it would have fallen under the mandates; clothes were either recycled or reused from previous productions or they were made out of fabric that already existed in the studio's costume shops and were therefore un-rationed. In the majority of films made during WWII, Hollywood created a reflection of the every-day world that men and women were living in with a touch of glamour.

In Warner Brother's famous 1942 film, *Casablanca*, producer Hal Wallis was concerned about the use of overly dressed up clothing for the characters, particularly Ingrid Bergman. He sent an inter-office memo to director Michael Curtiz on June 3, 1942 stating:

> "There are a couple of new costume changes for INGRID BERGMAN, evening outfits, and I wish you would look at them and then talk to me. The outfits, in my opinion, are okay. I prefer the number 11 with just a clip instead of all the necklaces. But my point in writing you is that we should think seriously about

whether this girl should ever appear in an evening outfit. After all, these two people are trying to escape from the country. The Gestapo is after them; they are refugees, making their way from country to country, and they are not going to Rick's café for social purposes. It seems a little incongruous to me for her to dress up in evening clothes as though she carried a wardrobe with her. I think it would be better for Henreid to wear a plain sport outfit, or a palm beach suit, and if she wore just a plain little street suit. Somehow or other these evening costumes seem to rub me the wrong way…" (Wallis).

Figure 14: Ingrid Bergman in *Casablanca*, wearing a White suit with Clip Broach, 1943, Hollywood.

This was one of several memos regarding the looks of the characters at "Rick's Café" in *Casablanca*; Wallis was insistent on the clothing being as realistic as possible. (see fig. 14)

In the Warner Brothers Archives there is a report from "*Movieland*" about the photographer Henry Waxman, who talks about shooting pin-up girls during the war for the boys in the military. "For the most part, the boys don't seem to want the girls glamorized too much…They prefer them to look natural- like the pretty girl down the block they dated before they went to war" (JH). That sentiment is an idea that Hollywood studio executives embraced as well due to pressures from the War Department and the pressure to make a profit.

When the U.S. entered the war in 1941, the War Department expanded its bounds into the movie industry. It created an office through the War Production Board (WPB) aptly named the Motion Picture and Photographic Section of the Consumer Durable Goods Division. It had two main offices- one in Washington, D.C. and one in Hollywood. The purpose of this office was to review all films and photographs made in Hollywood to make sure they did not undermine the image the WPB wanted to project to the public and to make sure that where rationing was required, it was being adhered to across the board in all departments (i.e. Props, Scenery, Film Stock, Wardrobe, etc.).

In September, 1942, Arch Reeve of the Public Relations Committee of the Motion Picture Industry reported on the status of Hollywood and the war effort. When figures were looked at regarding conservation efforts in the industry, the results showed "that substitutes have been found for nineteen vital materials without affecting the quality of production and that large quantities of steel, copper, aluminum, brass, bronze, rubber, and other critical supplies have thus been conserved for the war program" (Reeve).

The executives of the large studios took great strides to conserve materials for the war effort and to show the public films that reflected the stance the U.S. and U.K were taking against the Axis Powers and the war. The Motion Picture Association of America (MPAA) released a report early in the war, presumably 1942--- no date is listed on the report except that it was in June--- that discusses the effect of the war on Hollywood. It is a very positive and upbeat report, if not sometimes insulting to the Japanese population of America at the time, and discusses the Wardrobe Departments' issues as well. He spoke of the conservation efforts that were put into effect and how it "These new things will be in tune with the times, serve their purpose equally well or better than the old, and what is most important of all fit into the savings efforts of our country" (MPAA report on the Effect of War on Hollywood).

The importance of conserving materials and also meeting the mandates of the War Production Board were noted in his report as well: "Wardrobe departments in Hollywood's big studios were quick to meet the challenge. There is still a hold-over supply of the heavy cloth materials used to make the so-called "oomph" costumes, but creative designers are turning more and more to lighter, frillier materials and are getting even more "oomph" in their dresses" (MPAA report on the Effect of War on Hollywood).

For sports and casual wear, cotton had been popular. The change that appeared with WWII was its cross-over into evening wear and suits. "It is patriotic to wear cotton, and besides, the designers say, there are untold possibilities for glamour in this material. Bring in enough contrast with cotton, they point out, and you've got something refreshingly modern. Use patterned materials and pick it up with bright, startling costume jewelry and you are going to have something which will excite the imagination of every theatre-goer" (MPAA report on the Effect of War on Hollywood).

In the area of makeup, Max Factor and the House of Westmore, were working overtime to continue to create the defining looks of the decade. Included in the creations with makeup are special effects. "With rubber pieces for "character" makeup as scarce as Japs in Hollywood something had to be done in the laboratories. Synthetic skin pieces were invented and other forms of plastic were made that now serve better than rubber" (MPAA report on the Effect of War on Hollywood). The special effects sector of makeup application had always been a constantly changing and progressing art. The use of synthetics in the creation of prosthetic pieces was just one of the innovations to come of the war in the beauty industry.

The recurring theme in all the documents concerning the war and fashion is that of support for the war effort and maintaining beauty and morale being of utmost importance. The image here is an example of the dual advertising that was commonplace during the war. (see fig. 15) Magazines and propaganda posters emphasized to women that they could lift

Figure 15: Makeup Advertisement for Elizabeth Arden, c. 1943, Courtesy of the Advertising Archives.

morale by making sure they were in makeup and their hair was styled to the best of their ability. "With a political incorrectness unimaginable today, government, business, and charity all acknowledged that American GIs were virile, mostly working-class males. If a GI needed encouragement in tough times, he wanted it to come from a woman like [Betty] Grable, who famously said, 'I'm strictly an enlisted man's girl'" (Stanchak). Women, constantly encouraged to maintain their beauty even though they were working in jobs where they would be filthy by the time they ended their day, were influenced by Hollywood. Hollywood encouraged this by having the starlets of the day advertise products used on set and in their daily lives. This was the beginning of such advertisements in any large capacity. Companies such as Max Factor had an amazing clientele of celebrities that participated in ads for them. Max Factor had been in Hollywood since 1908 and created the first flexible grease paint for film that wouldn't crack or melt on camera under the hot lights. (see fig. 16)   He opened his line of cosmetics to the public in 1920 and coined the system of "Color Harmony" in which different shades of

Figure 16: Max Factor Advertisement, c. 1943, Hollywood, CA.

cosmetics complimented ladies of differing hair color and skin tone. He was considered the most successful makeup artist in Hollywood at the time and when the public saw his advertisements, they paid attention. The line of thought hoped for was that if the stars were using his cosmetics on the silver screen, then they must be good enough to use in a factory so the ladies could look like a million bucks all day long.

To encourage sales and keep morale high, cosmetic companies created names for products such as "Victory Red". Other names included "Auxiliary Red" and "Jeep Red" lipstick by Tussy and a red nail polish by Cutex named "Alert." As mentioned in the "*Movieland*" release, makeup for the legs became popular as silk stockings and nylon stockings were not available. (see fig. 17)

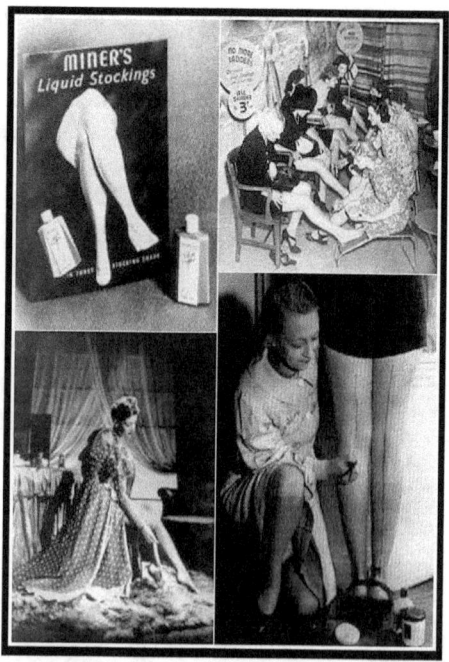

Figure 17: "Liquid" Stockings, courtesy of Simonleblanc.com

Cosmetic packaging was something else that began to change in the late 1930's and definitely by the start of the war. With the conservation effort in full force, especially to conserve metals, the cosmetics industry had to figure out how to package their products in a new way and they found it in the new, all man-made synthetics, particularly plastics. Where once powders, rouges, and lipsticks came in nickel, tin, or aluminum type packaging, there was now a shift to plastics taking place. Everything from powder, lipstick, cold cream, mascara- all of it went into plastic containers. (see figures 18 and 19)

Figure 18: Above: Before- Max Factor Packaging made of metal and glass, c. 1935. Photo taken at the Max Factor Museum, Hollywood, CA

Figure 19: After: Max Factor Packaging made mostly of plastic, c. 1942. Photo taken at the Max Factor Museum, Hollywood, CA.

One British company, Cyclex, changed its packaging to cardboard, especially for powders. "The Cyclax Company also did its bit for the war effort by issuing standard service beauty kits to servicewomen which included 'Auxiliary Red' lipstick in cylinders which were specifically designed to fit uniform pockets" (Wagga Wagga Museum of the Riverina, Cyclax Face Powder). Another product of note was Tangee lipstick. When speaking with Alice Joyce Lee who was 15 in 1943 in Mobile, Alabama, she remembers "…I could wear a touch of color on my lips when I went into town. Tangee was cheap and it changed color according to your skin tone so it wasn't too brash or bold and looked quite natural" (Lee). Across the Atlantic Ocean, women of Britain were also wearing Tangee after seeing advertisements about the naturalness of the product which emphasized the importance of looking beautiful. It is interesting to note the emphasis on recycling packaging at the bottom of the advertisement; this was common during the war. (see fig. 20)

Figure 20: British Ad for "Tangee" Lip color, c. 1943, London.

Hair in Hollywood was a big deal; it needed to look lustrous, vibrant, and healthy to show that on the home-front, be it in the U.S. or Britain, people were strong and healthy which in turns meant they will win the war. The practicality of hair care did change however. Women had to conserve their beauty products due to limited production of certain items, such as glycerin and shampoo, and because of the limited production of packaging. Women would use soap flakes or plain tap water to clean their hair.

This is one of the reasons head scarves, turbans, and hats became so popular during WWII. It was a glamorous way of hiding not so glamorous hair. The second reason was for safety. With women now working in factories with welding and moving machinery, their hair could easily get caught or get burned and so scarves and turbans became essential. Beauty tips in magazines included:

-Use vegetable dye for hair color to touch up your roots.

-If you have run out of lipstick, use beet juice to stain your lips.

-Use lipstick on your cheeks as well as your lips for added color.

-Need a tan? Use brown gravy as a self-tanner.

-Recycle your hair pins. If you need an up-do, bring your own pins to the salon

-Roll your own hair if you need to- use scrap rag

pieces instead of rollers.

Figure 21: Betty Grable in "Victory Rolls", c. 1943.

The most famous hair style to come out of WWII was that of the "Victory Rolls." (see fig. 21) It was a hairstyle which allowed women to get their hair up, out of their face and off their neck if they worked in a factory. It consisted of barrel rolls in the front and either loose curls in the back or the back would be held up in a snood. A snood is a type of hair net; however it is generally crocheted and heavier and came in all different colors and styles to add flair and creativity to a lady's individual style. (see fig. 22) Other ways women got around the shortage of hair products was to steam their hair over a bowl of water in order to break up the

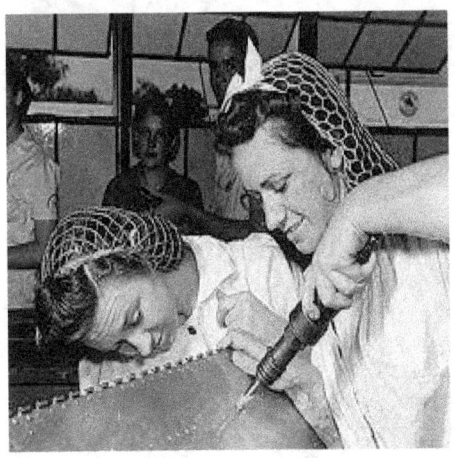

Figure 22: Factory workers wearing Snoods, c. 1942.

oils and dirt and then scrub their scalp with a towel.

Hollywood also influenced New York and Broadway in fashion and image. Both cities had a "canteen" in which servicemen could come, dance, drink and socialize with celebrities, all at no charge. It was usually for servicemen coming into port from overseas. The importance of the canteens is that the stars were not entering the canteens costumed and made up. They were coming in as regular people who happened to carry with them the latest trends in Hollywood and these trends transcended the canteen and made their ways into magazines and homes of the every-day woman. When women could see that Marlene Dietrich and Katharine Hepburn really did wear trousers with panache, they followed suit.

In Hollywood, it was aptly named the "Hollywood Canteen", founded by Bette Davis and John Garfield. (see fig. 23)

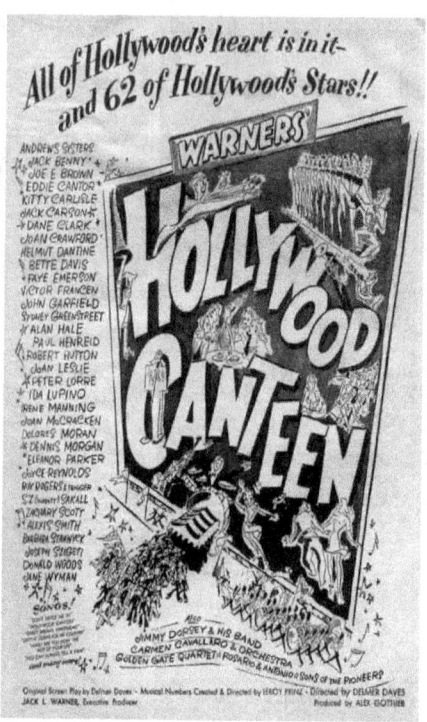

Figure 23: Ad for *Warner's Hollywood Canteen*, c. 1944, Hollywood.

The Hollywood Canteen was open from October 3, 1942 to November 22, 1945, and had celebrity volunteers such as Joan Crawford, Barbara Stanwyck, Alan Hale, and Ida Lupino. Entertainment was provided by such greats as Jimmy Dorsey and The Andrew Sisters, along with famous comedians like Jack Benny. Warner Bros. eventually made a film in 1944, *Hollywood Canteen*, so that non-military persons could also feel like they could mingle with the stars.

The New York version of the canteen was named the "Stage Door Canteen" and offered the same services provided by celebrity volunteers mostly from Broadway. Celebrities such as Tallulah Bankhead, Katharine Hepburn, Harpo Marx, Bing Crosby and Ethel Merman, to name a few, sang and danced, served drinks and food, and kept the servicemen on their way in or out of New York City entertained for free.

The Stage Door Canteen operated from March 1, 1942 to the end of 1945. Perks such as the two millionth guest winning tickets to the new hit *Oklahoma!* on Broadway were not uncommon. Money came in from private donations and Irving Berlin even wrote a song called "I Left My Heart at the Stage Door Canteen" for the film *This is the Army* in which all the proceeds went to the canteen. *Stage Door Canteen*, the film, was also created for the rest of the world to see. (see fig. 24)

Figure 24: *Stage Door Canteen* Movie Poster, Sol Lesser Productions, 1943.

Segregation did not exist in the canteens either; All servicemen were equal among the stars. In *Stage Door Canteen*, one of the girls, Irene, is going to be married, and instead of a lavish dress she is wearing a simple suit and beautiful floral hat with a small veil. This was the type of clothing worn during the war and it was important to see it on the big screen.

The costuming of the plays and musicals during this period was either contemporary dress or they were over the top with fringe, pattern, and color. The theatre houses that did remain open on Broadway were doing the same thing the Hollywood studios were in that they were recycling material, costumes, and scenery to the best of their ability. From my research, Broadway seems to have reacted in the same way as Hollywood in its conservation efforts and fundraising.

It is hard to say how big of an impact the entertainment industry had on fashion during WWII because its reach was so wide and so influential. Millions of men and women went to the movies and read magazines during the war and took from it the beauty and looks of its women and men and tried desperately to replicate them, much as people still do today. The support for the war effort shown by Hollywood and Broadway was immense and shaped the look of the Golden Age of Cinema and of women around the world.

Chapter Four

The Beginning of a Synthetic Revolution in Fashion

The new fabrics created during this time are still used today in clothing, household, mechanical, and everyday items. Most synthetics, when used in clothing, are a blend of two or more materials and have gone through many years of research to make telling the difference between a synthetic and a raw material almost impossible. This period in history and the needs it presented are responsible for the innovative research and creation of materials used to help the war effort and also ones that consumers could not conceive of not using today.

Stephen Fenichell notes in his book *Plastic*: the first plastics were made from cellulose-pure vegetable fibers. Henry Ford made plastics from soybeans. In the 1920's Germans made plastic from cows blood which came from abattoirs (9). The term "plastic" was derived from the Latin *plasticas* which means "that may be molded." Plastic came to be a term that encompassed any group of synthetic or semi-synthetic polymers which were usually known also by their brand name (e.g. *Rayon, Nylon, Bakelite*, etc.)

Synthetic materials were not completely new to the world. At the end of the 19th century, in 1855, *Viscose* was created. It was the first "man-made" fiber and was patented in 1892. However, it is important to note that *Viscose* is not an entirely man-made synthetic. It is a semi-synthetic. Made of wood cellulose, a naturally occurring polymer, mixed with chemicals to produce a fiber that could be used in textiles. *Viscose* was commercially produced in the U.K. as early as 1910 and it became commercially produced in in the U.S. in 1924. After a competition for a new name for *Viscose* in 1924 in the U.S., the name *Rayon* was given to *Viscose* for U.S. consumers (Haldane). Many designers used it as a substitute for silk as it had a high luster and lightweight feel.

DuPont is credited as the American forerunner of the plastics industry. Before 1920 the company had been producing gun and blasting powders when they turned their interests to cellophane. DuPont built a factory in Buffalo, New York that would produce *Viscose* and built a cellophane factory next door as well. In 1924 the first sheet of cellophane came off the press but was a failure because it could not hold up to moisture. In 1926, after implementing a 4 part system which kept moisture out of the cellophane, cellophane packaging was created. It was used by candy manufacturers as well as clothing designers. For example, designer Elsa Schiaparelli (1890-1973) worked with the Colcombet Company to create her "Glass" cape which was made using a form of cellophane called *Rhodophane*. It wasn't a commercial success as the fabric dissolved when dry cleaned, but its unconventional nature rocked the fashion world. (see fig. 25)

Figure 25: Elsa Schiaparelli's "Glass Cape", 1934, Paris.

In an attempt to make *Rayon* more commercially versatile and viable for use in fashion, DuPont decided to de-luster *Rayon*, which it did successfully by adding titanium oxide, a white paint pigment. This new form of *Rayon* was a hit with French couture designers including Elsa Schiaparelli. She used the fabric to create form-fitting evening gowns in the 1930's.

With the success of *Rayon*, DuPont was on the hunt for a purely synthetic fiber that would one day replace silk hosiery. The company wooed Harvard chemist Wallace Hume Corothers to join DuPont to create such a fiber. Carothers left Harvard and began research at DuPont in 1927 in its Pure Science Division. He was able to do research without limits. Carothers said "…as for funds, the sky is the limit. I can spend as much as I please" (Fenchinell159). Carothers' understanding of his position at DuPont when joining was that he would be involved in all aspects of research and development of fibers he created. After years of research Carothers and his colleague Julian Hill discovered the beginnings of what today is called *Nylon*. The New York Times touted "Chemists Produce Synthetic Silk" on September 2, 1931. Carothers and Hill had produced what they called "cold-drawing" where "a clump of filaments rolled into a small ball and compressed showed a remarkable springiness resembling wool. In their elastic properties, these fibers are very much superior to any know artificial silk…The experiments recently conducted clearly demonstrated for the first time the possibility of obtaining useful fibers from a strictly synthetic material" (Fenichell 167). This would be of great importance in the coming years when raw materials would be unavailable due to the war.

The original "synthetic silk" produced by Carothers was too expensive to manufacture at the time. Also, it had a low melting point which would be problematic for the average consumer when they had the material cleaned or if they were exposed to extreme heat. After more research, finally in 1934, *Fiber 66* was created. Carothers had created a super polymer that could be cold drawn and had a melting point of 195 degrees. DuPont had Carothers continue his research in this area, while the company took him and his team out of the loop concerning mass production. Essentially, Carothers felt DuPont had wooed him away from Harvard to create a product no one else could and then dropped him when they no longer needed his research. Carothers, who was known to have had serious bouts of depression, sank into his deepest depression to date which was sparked by his removal from a key component of his work. DuPont sent him on a mandatory vacation to try and improve his mental health. During this time his sister died. Wallace Carothers killed himself on April 29, 1937; the irony is he did so by ingesting cyanide.

Fiber 66 underwent a name contest as well and the winner was *Nylon*. Silk stockings were being purchased by women at a rate of 500 million pairs a year by 1938. That translated to an estimated $700 million to Japanese silk producers alone (Fenichell). DuPont was very aware of the market and knew that working women could be counted on to run through 36 pairs of silk stockings in one year.

Nylon stockings were finally introduced to the world at the New York World's Fair in April 1939. (see fig. 26)

Figure 26: Poster for the New York World Fair, 1939.

The Philadelphia Record published this headline the day after the unveiling: "*New Synthetic Fiber May Smash Jap Monopoly*" (Fenchinell 138). The first trial sale of *Nylons* was in Wilmington, Delaware. Women were only allowed 3 pair per customer and had to provide a local address to which the stockings would be delivered as they were not permitted take them out of the store. Women came from all over the country, renting hotel rooms so they would have a valid address. The cost was $1.15, $1.25, and $1.35 per pair depending on the gauge. The average cost of silk stockings at the time was $0.79. All 4,000 pairs of the new *Nylon* stockings sold out. That year, *Nylon* even appeared for the first time in a movie: it was used in "*The Wizard of Oz*" to create the tornado that whisked Dorothy to the Emerald City (Uffner).

After a great trial run of the new *Nylon* stocking and after making the general public wait over a year, on May 15, 1940 or "N-Day", the first national test and sale happened. The availability of the new stocking was to be short lived. After the bombing of Pearl Harbor in 1941, *Nylon* was pulled from the commercial market and was supplied exclusively to the military for war purposes, particularly for parachutes as well as tents, ropes, and some rain-gear. With its inherent properties of being abrasion resistant, exceptionally strong, lustrous, and low in moisture absorbency among several, *Nylon's* exclusivity with the military would last until the end of the war. When it was available once again to the public, it was a massive success.

Chapter Five

Designers that Made an Impact during the War

Before WWII began most of the famous designers had design houses in Paris, France. Paris was the fashion capital of the world and created couture, or custom-made, clothing for the most prominent figures in society. There were designers in the late 1920's that began to make a name for themselves by creating clothing for the elite as well as the everyday woman. There are notably six I will discuss here, as they had a huge impact on fashion leading up to WWII and even after Paris was occupied by the Nazi regime. They are: Gabrielle "Coco" Chanel (1883-1971), Elsa Schiaparelli (1890-1973), Adrian (1903-1959), Mainbocher (1890-1976), Arnold Lever, and Edith Head (1897-1981). Their importance lie in the fact that they contributed to women's wear during the war by influencing the looks of the "working class" woman by the textiles they wore and the imagination that adorned their heads in the work of millinery- one of the few places extravagances could live. They not only dressed the masses but created some of the most beautiful garments for the stars of Hollywood. These designers helped bridge the gap between the ever disseminating classes and reflected in clothing the rise of the middle class during WWII.

Coco Chanel's designing career began as a milliner. She designed hats to suit her own simple, elegant tastes. When they caught attention from the public, after being worn by famous actresses in Paris, she began to branch out into designing clothing. However, her designs were free from the restraint of the heavy corsets and binding undergarments that exemplified the time. They draped the body, had a lowered waist, and often were made of light-weight fabrics, making ease of movement a priority. Women loved them and critics loved to hate them. Initially, the social elite found her designs brought common peasantry and working

Figure 27: Coco Chanel (left) and a friend wearing her Jersey Knit Suit.

class design to the world of the fashionable. She used jersey knit fabric to create the first Jersey Knit Suit, which also showed women's ankles. (see fig. 27) Most of her early designs were for day, casual, wear and work wear as more women had stepped into the working world because of WWI. Bathing suits, pants, and jersey knit jackets were also some of the firsts she created in her casual line of wear. She designed evening wear that was just as comfortable, yet used chiffons, silks and tulle to soften the silhouette and make a more feminine statement. Throughout the 1930's she had a successful career and even was hired by Samuel Goldwyn in 1931 to travel to Hollywood to design couture outfits for the stars of MGM such as Katharine Hepburn. Chanel was the creator of the first "Little Black dress" that, to this day, is a staple in women's wardrobes. (see fig. 28)

Figure 28: Coco Chanel's "Little Black Dress", 1926, Paris.

Another aspect of Chanel was the sensationalism that surrounded her throughout her life. "The international economic depression of the 1930s had a negative impact on her company, but it was the outbreak of World War II that led Chanel to close her business. She fired her workers and shut down her shops. During the German occupation of France, Chanel became involved with a German military officer, Hans Gunther von Dincklage. She got special permission to stay in her apartment at the Hotel Ritz, however, she did move to southern France where she made pullovers for soldiers and lived a relatively quiet life. After the war ended, Chanel was interrogated by her relationship with von Dincklage, but she was not charged as a collaborator.

Some have wondered whether her friend Winston Churchill worked behind the scenes on her behalf. While not officially charged, Chanel suffered in the court of public opinion. Some still viewed her relationship with a Nazi officer as a betrayal of her country. Chanel left Paris, spending some years in Switzerland in a sort of exile. She also lived at her country house in Roquebrune for a time" (Biography.com).

She did not return to fashion until 1954 when she made a successful comeback with her signature Chanel Suit and the use of inexpensive imitation pearl necklaces. She delved into the world of perfume and created the famous "Chanel No. 5" beginning a still-growing part of her company. Coco Chanel's impact on fashion in the 1920's and 1930's left an indelible mark on the fashion world in the ways of fabric choice, liberation of movement in clothing for women, and designing completely out of the box.

Elsa Schiaparelli (1890-1973), an Italian designer who made her name in Paris, was another pioneer in women's fashion and also a "rival" of Coco Chanel. While Chanel had a more understated and streamlined aesthetic, Schiaparelli was famous for her use of textiles and shocking designs. She was good friends with many artists in Paris, including Jean Cocteau and Alberto Giacometti, as well as Salvador Dali with whom she collaborated with on some of her most famous designs. (see fig. 29)

Figure 29: Bow-knot Sweater, Hand-knit pullover sweater with bow-knot, November 1927, Black and White Wool, by Elsa Schiaparelli.

Her first big break came when she designed a simple double knit sweater that had the illusion of a scarf tied in a bow. In 1930, Schiaparelli introduced the use of the zipper in women's dresses. These were used up until 1939-1940, when the metal used for the zippers was recalled for war materials. Dresses then returned to using buttons as fasteners until the end of the war, or when she could, she would use plastic zippers.

Both she and American designer Vera Max are credited with being the first to create the jumpsuit for women; Schiaparelli is credited with creating the "siren suit" used for air raids in Britain. The "siren suit" was complete with a gas mask, a flask, and a turban to cover un-presentable hair, as the women were expected to be torn from bed. She was a visionary and an innovator, looking at all aspects of design and textiles.

One of the first to use the new world of man-made synthetics in her clothing and apply bold prints to them added appeal and edge; she introduced Rayon as fabric for evening gowns in the mid 1930's. Her collaboration with the Colcombet Company in France produced many exciting and new designs using synthetic fabrics such as Rayon, Acrylic, and Rayon with metal threads called "Fildifer". This would prove fortunate when Paris became occupied by the Nazis, she left for New York City where she continued to design during the war. Her knowledge and willingness to incorporate synthetics into her designs only enhanced her popularity and sales during the war.

Figure 30: "Shoe Hat" by Elsa Schialparelli, collaboration with Salvador Dali, Black Wook Felt, 1937-38.

Hats would come to play an important role during WWII as there were very few, if any, rationing limitations set for millinery. Schiaparelli's hats were extraordinary and surreal, reflecting her personal life which was surrounded by artists. (see fig. 30) One of the more "tame" hats she introduced was the turban in 1930's. This invention would become a valuable asset to women's clothing during WWII, as it covered their heads when working in factories and protected them from fumes and accidents, and also served women by allowing them femininity on the job. Women could find their individual character through hats and used them to set themselves apart when their wardrobe could not.

Some of her other major innovations include:

- Surrealist fashions, like erotic-shaped hats, food-looking accessories, fabrics printed with body parts, bones and organs, and even household furniture, so your breasts looked like a bureau drawer.

- Ethnic themed collections including the popular Turban hat popular in the late 1930's and early 1940's.

- Culottes, which was a skirt divided to make long flowing shorts, popularized by famous tennis player Lili de Alvarez who wore them at Wimbledon in 1931.

- Water-proof cotton.

- The wrap around dress.

Schiaparelli was a forerunner of avant-garde fashion and allowed women to indulge in their artistic fancy. After WWII Schiaparelli returned to Paris and found it had changed from the Paris she knew and understood. She closed her design house in 1954. Schiaparelli died in 1973.

Adrian, born Adrian Adolph Greenburg (1903-1959), was a combination of an influential Hollywood designer before WWII and a custom dress designer during WWII. In his early career he designed for Broadway and then worked for Cecile B. DeMille's private film production company. He moved to Los Angeles with DeMille's company and joined MGM as Chief Costume Designer in 1928. There he influenced fashion around the world by creating and popularizing some of the most memorable costume designs in history.

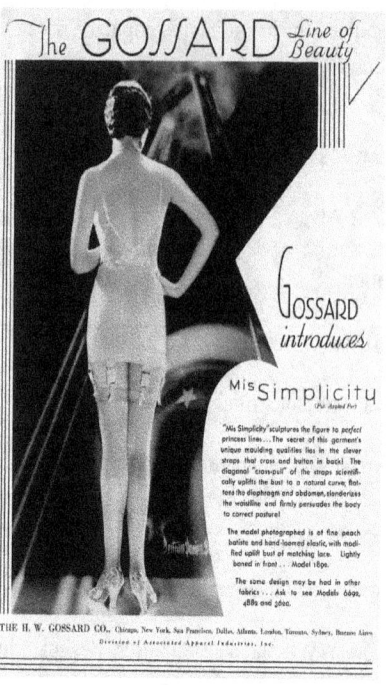

Figure 31: Vintage Advertisement for the Gossard Line of Beauty, c. 1931.

In fashion, the 1930's brought the invention of a women's corset that was made of rubber and silk, with little or no boning. (see fig. 31) This allowed women to complete the look of the time by having soft curves and flattened breasts without being as uncomfortable as they were in previous years with stiff boning. These corsets also allowed women to wear the new bias cut dresses created by Madeleine Vionnet (1876-1975), which gently wrapped around the figure showing off its curves. Backless dresses were also introduced in the 1930's, being attributed to Hollywood designer Adrian who designed the dresses for Greta Garbo, which required the aforementioned rubber and silk corset because it tended to have the deep back to accommodate such dresses.

Perhaps his most popular look created in the 1930's was the *Letty Lynton* dress designed for Joan Crawford in 1932. (see fig. 32) Macy's sold over half a million copies of the dress after the film premiered. "The design, which emphasized Crawford's naturally broad shoulders, has been widely credited with setting the vogue for the shoulder pad..." (Mendes and de la Haye). He is most well-known for his designs in *The Wizard of Oz* (1939), including the ruby slippers.

Figure 32: Joan Crawford in *Letty Lynton*, Designed by Adrian, 1932, Hollywood.

In 1941 Adrian left MGM and began his own line of custom made dresses. "In January, 1942, his first collection was shown at the May Company department store in Los Angeles. Unsuccessful at first, Adrian held another show the following month and was soon selling his designs in department stores across the USA. His ready to wear line carried the "Adrian Original" label and his couture clothing was labeled "Adrian Custom". To remain exclusive, he allowed only one store in each city to sell his collections" (Zappitelli).

His contribution during the war was important because it lent a sense of glamour to the rationed streamlined look of WWII women's clothing. (see fig. 33) His women's suits were well tailored, with eye-catching fabric inserts which made it more appealing to the mass number of women who were entering the professional workforce due to the war; they could look feminine and business-like at the same time. Adrian's popularity during the 1930's was extremely helpful to his sales in the 1940's. He died unexpectedly in 1959 of a heart attack.

Figure 33: Suit by Adrian, c. 1944, Hollywood.

Mainbocher (pronounced MAIN-BAWKER, as opposed to a French pronunciation), originally named Main Rousseau Bocher, made a name for himself in Paris before the war even though he is American. Born in Connecticut, he stayed in France after serving in WWI and worked for *Harper's Bazaar*, afterward becoming the editor of French *VOGUE* magazine. In 1929 he created his own line of couture garments and opened a store in Paris. There, his designs created a buzz of elegance and extravagance for the next decade. As did other designers in Paris, he moved his store to New York when the war began in 1939. He opened a fashion house next to Tiffany's on 57th street in Manhattan and continued to have success in America.

Mainbocher's contribution to fashion during WWII was significant. His line consisted only of *haute couture* fashion, or completely custom made clothing, whereas other designers had a ready-to-wear line as well. His line catered to the social elite both in Paris and New York. However, he did design the uniforms for the U.S. Navy WAVES (Women Accepted for Voluntary Emergency Service) in 1942, which was tailored and strong, while still showing the curves of the women wearing the uniforms. (see fig. 34)

Figure 34: Mainbocher's Uniform Design for the U.S. Navy's WAVES, 1942.

In addition to the regular uniform, Mainbocher created a summer version of the WAVES uniform in gray so the women would stay cooler. The uniform was also adopted by the SPARS (Women's Reserve of the Coast Guard). These uniforms were considered the best and sharpest looking uniforms in the military for women and were touted as so when recruiting women for service. Mainbocher continued to find success throughout the war with the social elite and even designed the new women's U.S.M.C. (United States Marine Corps) uniform in 1952. After the war, Mainbocher stayed in New York and worked until he closed his doors in 1971.

Other fashion designers of the time contributed to the war by creating uniforms as well. Bergdorf Goodman designed the uniform for the WASP (Women's Airforce Service Pilots) in a

Santiago blue gabardine that came to be popular with the pilots. The uniform had several versions including one for dress, and one for flying. (see fig. 35)

Figure 35: WASP Uniforms, c. 1944, courtesy of the Army Air Corps Library and Museum.

The flying version employed the "Eisenhower" jacket, named after Dwight D. Eisenhower, and slacks. The "Eisenhower" jacket was a popular men's jacket that was designed with a cropped waist and large pleating in the back to accompany insulating layers beneath it. The dress uniform was made up of a belted jacket and skirt with a beret which was designed by Frederick's of Hollywood.

In addition to designers of uniforms and dresses, Arnold Lever was a textiles designer in London working for Jacqmar. Jacqmar was a famous scarf company founded in 1932. "The firm was established by Joseph "Jack" Lyons with his wife Mary. The company had offices and a showroom at 16 Grosvenor Street in London's Mayfair. The founders had, typically, "Frenchified" their names from Jack and Mary to create a sense of glamour suited to a high class Mayfair fashion house. An advertisement for Jacqmar from *VOGUE* announces their "Spring 1942 Collection" and places their silk and tweed products as an alternative to the French designs that were no longer internationally available" (Rennie 12). Lever was the company's designer and began to design propaganda scarves during the war. The propaganda was divided into three categories: Friends, Victory, and Service. (see fig. 36)

Figure 36: "Salvage Your Rubber", Jacqmar Propaganda Scarf, early 1940's, Paul and Karen Renny Collection.

Though the designs were never directly endorsed by any political powers, they were worn by celebrities, the social elite, everyday women, and factory workers. The factory workers in particular wore them as a safety precaution to protect their hair, but with their symbolic and patriotic messages, they were a very popular accessory. Lever went on to open his own design studio in 1947.

In terms of practicality, Edith Head was one of the most successful designers for Hollywood films before and during WWII. Born as Edith Posener, she became known professionally as Edith Head after her marriage to Charles Head in 1923. Although they divorced in 1936, she retained her name. She began working for Paramount Pictures in 1923 by deception. Applying for a design assistant position, she was hired as just that for the costume department of Paramount Pictures by using another's sketches in the interview. She did eventually learn to draw under the guidance of her boss Howard Greer who was said to have found her deception "hilarious" (Ducey).

She would work for Paramount Pictures for 44 years before moving to Universal Pictures in 1967, where she worked until her death in 1981. During her time at Paramount, Head was renowned for coming in under budget and on time with her designs, as well as making her leading men and ladies happy. When the U.S. entered the war and the studios went to work creating both realistic and escapist films, Head was indispensable as a designer who saved the studio money and still managed to have beautiful costumes.

Recycling of costumes was not new to Head; she was extremely familiar with the inventory of the Paramount costume warehouse. For pre-war productions she would pull a large amount of stock from the warehouse and make changes to the existing clothing for the supporting characters, bit players, and extras. This way of working became imperative during the war. With rationing of new materials in effect, Head had a whole warehouse of costumes and pre-war un-rationed bolts of fabric to choose from for new costumes that had more panache.

Figure 37: Veronica Lake in the Night Gown designed by Edith Head for *I Married a Witch*, 1942.

One of the films she costumed during the war was *I Married a Witch* starring Veronica Lake and Frederic March. (see fig. 37) The black evening dress Lake wears in the end of the film is a great example of the simplicity of the new war-time silhouette, yet the beauty and genius of Head's design is apparent. Using material not readily available to the public any longer capitalized on Lake's sexy onscreen persona, inspired women to maintain their own beauty at home, and contributed to the iconic images of Lake throughout her career. The dress, if it was to be made for consumers, would have had less material in the skirt, would have been shorter, and would have no lace on the bodice. An alternative look could be accomplished, with the inspiration Head created. She was the example studios looked for when hiring designers during the war.

Edith Head would continue to create costumes at Paramount for future classic films such as *Blue Hawaii*, *Breakfast at Tiffany's* (Givenchy designed the gowns for this film), and *This Property is Condemned*. Her strong understanding of the human figure, especially women, helped to create some of the most beautiful and practical costumes in recent history.

The designers leading up to and during WWII were designers of imagination, ingenuity, and innovation. Taking the circumstances of the war they not only created beautiful garments, but created practical and iconic ones as well. Their designs have become a standard by which designers today look to for inspiration; their designs are always being recycled into new and exciting fashions. The uniforms designed brought grace and dignity to the women who wore them, while the civilian clothes worn were as beautiful as they were practical.

Conclusion

Fashion underwent a forced change in the 1940's and it bettered the industry as a whole, unifying designers for a common cause, unifying whole industries such as the Hollywood machine, and really utilized the use of propaganda in clothing for the first time. The impact on fashion, despite the limitations imposed upon it, was immense and is still felt today.

Rationing changed the face of fashion by placing new man-made materials and fibers in clothing. These fibers are still used today in mainstream fashion: *Nylon*, plastics, hemp, cotton and synthetic blends. The push created by the war to further research into the new materials helped to produce fibers such as *Lycra* and *Teflon*. Rationing also allowed for creativity within boundaries and popularized the ready-to-wear clothing market on a massive level.

With the limitations imposed on fashion, high fashion, and *couture* clothing took a backseat to more comfortable and practical clothing, including sportswear. Comfortable tops and pants were brought to the forefront, and today you cannot shop anywhere that does not contain a whole women's sportswear section, even having some clothing lines developed purely for sportswear purposes. If anything, today, more structured and high fashion clothing is worn only for special occasions or for the social elite.

New York City is considered one of the major fashion capitals of the world and has developed its persona in earnest since WWII. Had Paris not been occupied by the Nazi regime during WWII, this would not have happened as quickly as it did, nor would it have contained the designers originating from Paris and around the world to lend their talents to the city. London still maintains the reputation of being the land of well-made tailored clothing for men and women. In recent events such as the Royal wedding of Prince William, Britain has shown itself once again to the world as a millinery powerhouse. London never quite achieved the reputation it sought during the isolation of Paris as a high fashion go-to city, but it did retain an elegance and sophistication in accord with its long history of beautifully made clothing.

A bar was raised in women's independence through fashion during WWII. From the time women were involved in the war effort as early as 1939, and earlier in Britain, they helped designers to change the way women's clothing was perceived and achieved. Pants worn by women were looked upon with disdain and disapproval until it was recognized as a part of a type of uniform for the working woman. Pants went on to become even more popular in the following decades in leisure wear and in the creation of Capri short pants in the sixties. While maintaining beauty was socially of great importance in the media, the designs took the practical needs of women and infused them with beauty and grace, flattering every figure. The A-line dress, used in the government mandates in the U.S. and Britain proved to be a most beautiful line and to this day is considered one of the most flattering silhouettes for a woman of any shape and stature. After the war, women's fashion went into a very structured and bound silhouette with the "New Look", however, it did so with a fight. Women would express their independence again through fashion in the sixties by fighting against the constraints of clothing made in the fifties which, for many women, represented the repression of the independent woman.

In conclusion, the era was represented visually by the fashions of the time which made indelible marks on future designers and the science of fashion as we know it. Were it not for the events of WWII, many advances in fashion and technology would not have happened. With the innovations and inventions that came about, designers were able to create one of the most beautiful decades in history through fashion.